MEMORIAL DAY

LYNN HAMILTON

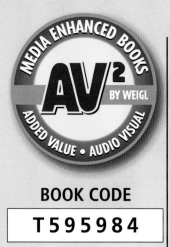

BOOK CODE

T 5 9 5 9 8 4

AV² **by Weigl** brings you media enhanced books that support active learning.

AV² provides enriched content that supplements and complements this book. Weigl's AV² books strive to create inspired learning and engage young minds for a total learning experience.

Go to **www.av2books.com**, and enter this book's unique code. You will have access to video, audio, web links, quizzes, a slide show, and activities.

Audio
Listen to sections of the book read aloud.

Video
Watch informative video clips

Web Link
Find research sites and play interactive games.

Try This!
Complete activities and hands-on experiments.

Due to the dynamic nature of the Internet, some of the URLs and activities provided as part of AV² by Weigl may have changed or ceased to exist. AV² by Weigl accepts no responsibility for any such changes. All media enhanced books are regularly monitored to update addresses and sites in a timely manner. Contact AV² by Weigl at 1-866-649-3445 or av2books@weigl.com with any questions, comments, or feedback.

Published by AV² by Weigl
350 5th Avenue, 59th Floor
New York, NY 10118
Website: www.av2books.com   www.weigl.com

Library of Congress Cataloging-in-Publication Data

Library of Congress Cataloging-in-Publication Data available upon request.
Fax 1-866-44-WEIGL for the attention of the Publishing Records department.

ISBN 978-1-60596-771-4 (hard cover)
ISBN 978-1-60596-778-3 (soft cover)

Printed in the United States of America in North Mankato, Minnesota
1 2 3 4 5 6 7 8 9 0 14 13 12 11 10

052010
WEP264000

Editor Heather C. Hudak   Design Terry Paulhus

Every reasonable effort has been made to trace ownership and to obtain permission to reprint copyright material. The publishers would be pleased to have any errors or omissions brought to their attention so that they may be corrected in subsequent printings.

Weigl acknowledges Getty Images as its primary image supplier for this book.
General John A. Logan Museum: page 8

CONTENTS

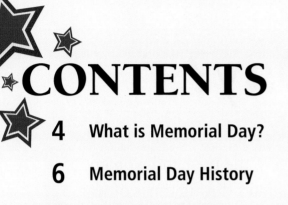

UNCOMMON
VALOR
WAS A COMMON
VIRTUE

What is Memorial Day?

Memorial Day is a national holiday that is observed on the last Monday in May. On this day, the men and women who died serving the United States during times of war are honored. It is also a time to honor the men and women who protect and defend the United States all year long.

On Memorial Day, **veterans**, military personnel, and citizens pay tribute to servicemen and women. Often, special ceremonies are held at **monuments** and cemeteries. Wreaths, flowers, and small U.S. flags are placed on the graves of fallen soldiers.

Some people quietly show their respect during private services. They think about the present-day soldiers and heroes who have served in the past.

Special Events
THROUGHOUT THE YEAR

JANUARY 1
NEW YEAR'S DAY

FEBRUARY (THIRD MONDAY)
PRESIDENTS' DAY

MARCH 17
ST. PATRICK'S DAY

SUNDAY IN MARCH OR APRIL
EASTER

MAY (LAST MONDAY)
MEMORIAL DAY

JUNE 14
FLAG DAY

JULY 4
INDEPENDENCE DAY

AUGUST (FIRST SUNDAY)
FAMILY DAY

SEPTEMBER (FIRST MONDAY)
LABOR DAY

OCTOBER (SECOND MONDAY)
COLUMBUS DAY

NOVEMBER 11
VETERANS DAY

DECEMBER 25
CHRISTMAS DAY

Memorial Day History

etween 1861 and 1865, the northern states fought against the southern states in the Civil War. The southern states wanted to become a separate nation. The northern states wanted to keep the country together. **Union** and Confederate soldiers fought many battles. About 500,000 soldiers died, and thousands more were wounded.

About 25 communities claim to have held the first memorial ceremony. Boalsburg, Pennsylvania, is one of these communities. In 1864, Emma Hunter and Sophie Keller met Elizabeth Meyers. All three women were visiting the graves of family members who had died during the Civil War. They agreed to meet again one year later. They planned to decorate the graves of all the soldiers who died during the Civil War. The following year, the whole town gathered to help them decorate the graves.

✯✯ Many American cities have Civil War monuments that honor the soldiers who fought in the war. The Pennsylvania Monument at the Gettysburg National Military Park is an example.

The Korean War Veterans War Memorial, in Washington, D.C., is dedicated to those who fought in the Korean War. Wreaths decorate the memorial on Memorial Day.

Henry Welles lived in Waterloo, New York. He thought a special day should be set aside each year to honor the fallen soldiers of the Civil War. General John B. Murray agreed with Welles's idea. The two men organized a memorial program. On May 5, 1866, businesses closed, and flags flew at **half-staff**. The village was decorated with black streamers and evergreen branches. The people of Waterloo visited nearby cemeteries to place crosses, flowers, and wreaths on the graves.

Past and Present Celebrations

MEMORIAL DAY was first known as Decoration Day because the graves of Civil War soldiers were decorated. **Arlington National Cemetery** continues to hold a Memorial Day celebration.

ABOUT 5,000 people attended the first Decoration Day. The same number of people still attend the ceremony.

TOWNS AND cities all over the country were celebrating Memorial Day by the late 1800s. Today, Memorial Day is a national holiday.

ON THE first celebration of Decoration Day, May 30, 1868, General James Garfield spoke at Arlington National Cemetery. Today, small U.S. flags are set on each grave. The president or vice-president gives a speech.

Important People

During the Civil War, General Jonathan Logan commanded the 31st Illinois Volunteer Infantry. After the Civil War ended, General Logan became a U.S. senator. He also led the Grand Army of the Republic, an organization for war veterans.

On May 5, 1868, Logan issued General Order No. 11. This order named May 30, 1868, as the official day to remember the fallen soldiers of the Civil War.

✮✮ General Logan's order explained how and why people should take part in ceremonies remembering fallen soldiers.

★★In 1993, President Bill Clinton approved the National World War II Memorial. The memorial, in Washington, D.C., honors the men and women who served in times of war and the citizens who supported the soldiers.

This is an excerpt from General Jonathan Logan's General Order No. 11.

"The 30th day of May, 1868, is designated for the purpose of strewing with flowers, or otherwise decorating the graves of **comrades** who died in defense of their country and during the late rebellion, and whose bodies now lie in almost every city, village, and hamlet churchyard in the land."

First-hand Account

"This weekend all across our country we gather to observe Memorial Day. Over this weekend we honor Americans from all our wars who died while defending our nation.

These brave men and women gave their tomorrows so that we might live in freedom. We must **vow** to uphold the ideals they died for and make our country great—an America free and strong, a force for peace and progress, a land of tolerance and opportunity for all."

In 1996, President Clinton gave this Memorial Day radio address.

Memorial Day Celebrations

Following General Logan's announcement, ceremonies took place in many communities. About 5,000 people attended the first official ceremony at Arlington National Cemetery in Virginia. Flowers were placed on more than 20,000 Union and Confederate graves.

In 1873, New York became the first state to name May 30 a legal holiday. Soon, many other states did the same. In 1882, May 30 was named Memorial Day. After World War I, people began to pay tribute to those who died serving in other wars as well.

⭐ On the Thursday before Memorial Day, soldiers of the 3ʳᵈ U.S. Infantry place small American flags at each of the more than 260,000 gravestones in Arlington National Cemetery. This has been a tradition since the late 1950s.

The U.S. government officially named Waterloo, New York, the "Birthplace of Memorial Day" in 1966. Many other observances had taken place 100 years before the ceremony in Waterloo. Still, Waterloo was the first city to hold a carefully planned event that involved an entire community. In 1971, Memorial Day was made a national holiday. Memorial Day activities were also moved to the last Monday in May—making the holiday part of a long weekend.

Memorial Day Around the World

CANADA

On November 11, Canadians celebrate Remembrance Day. This is a time to honor the men and women who have served the country in war and on peace missions.

MEXICO

On September 13, Los Niños Héroes honors the heroes of the Mexican-American War. The President of Mexico lays a wreath at the war monument in Chapultepec Park, in Mexico City.

FRANCE

The French celebrate Armistice Day on November 11. It is a day to remember those who served in World War I, as well as in other wars.

Celebrating Today

On Memorial Day, people across the United States show their respect for the men and women who have served in wars. Veterans and servicemen and women participate in parades and ceremonies. People visit cemeteries to place flowers, small flags, and wreaths on graves and monuments. Many ceremonies include memorial prayers, **patriotic** songs, and hymns. Often, "**Taps**" is played.

On Memorial day, flags are flown at half-staff on government buildings and ships across the country. During some ceremonies, flowers are strewn on the water to honor those who died at sea.

Ceremonies are held in Europe to honor the American soldiers who died in World War I and World War II. The Overseas Memorial Day Association organizes ceremonies and ensures that flags are placed on the graves of fallen soldiers buried overseas.

Since 1990, millions of viewers have watched the National Memorial Day Concert on television.

Memorial Day in the United States

Memorial Day ceremonies are held across the United States each May. Special ceremonies are held to remember the soldiers who were killed serving the country during times of war.

Oregon

OREGON Since 1945, the Fleet of Flowers has taken place in Depoe, Oregon. This event honors those who died during battles at sea. Thousands of people attend a ceremony on shore. Boats filled with flowers move from the harbor to the ocean. As military jets fly overhead, flowers and wreaths are tossed into the water.

HAWAI'I Ceremonies are held each year at the National Memorial Cemetery of the Pacific in Honolulu, Hawai'i. Before the ceremony, Boy Scouts decorate more than 33,000 graves with flags and **leis**. A service is also held at the USS *Arizona* Memorial to remember those who died in the 1941 attack on Pearl Harbor.

Hawai'i

Alaska

| 0 | 970 Miles |

| 0 | 1,278 Miles |

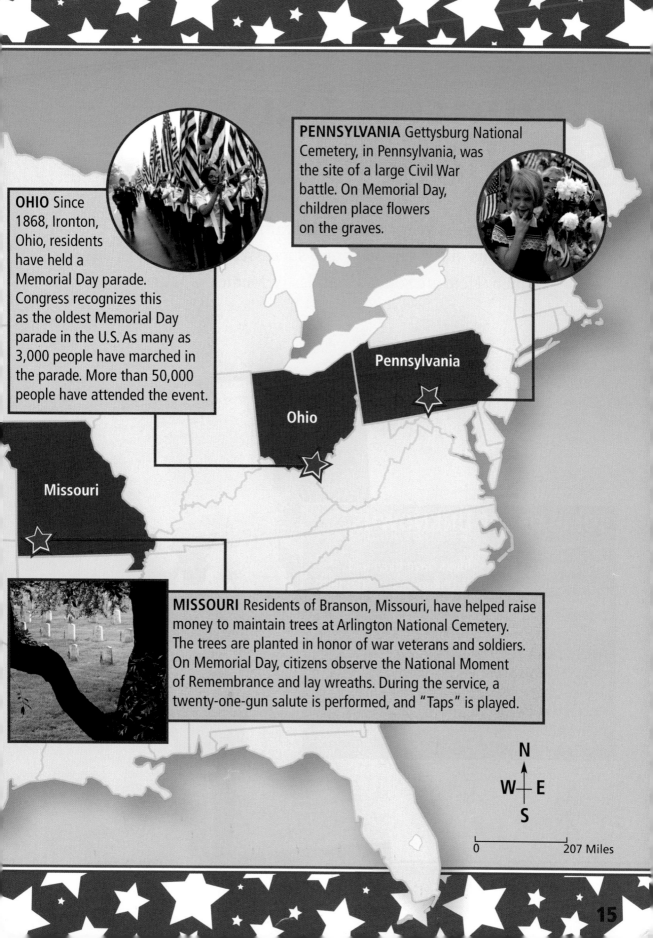

OHIO Since 1868, Ironton, Ohio, residents have held a Memorial Day parade. Congress recognizes this as the oldest Memorial Day parade in the U.S. As many as 3,000 people have marched in the parade. More than 50,000 people have attended the event.

PENNSYLVANIA Gettysburg National Cemetery, in Pennsylvania, was the site of a large Civil War battle. On Memorial Day, children place flowers on the graves.

MISSOURI Residents of Branson, Missouri, have helped raise money to maintain trees at Arlington National Cemetery. The trees are planted in honor of war veterans and soldiers. On Memorial Day, citizens observe the National Moment of Remembrance and lay wreaths. During the service, a twenty-one-gun salute is performed, and "Taps" is played.

Pennsylvania

Ohio

Missouri

N
W E
S

0   207 Miles

Memorial Day Symbols

Throughout the year, cemeteries, war museums, and monuments remind us of the sacrifices and successes of servicemen and women. Here are some examples of Memorial Day symbols.

TOMB OF THE UNKNOWNS

The remains of three soldiers have been laid to rest in the Tomb of the Unknowns at Arlington National Cemetery. One soldier fought in World War I, one soldier fought in World War II, and one soldier fought in the Korean War. The names of these three men are unknown. Together, they represent the many soldiers who have died while serving their country. On Memorial Day, the U.S. president places a wreath at the Tomb of the Unknowns.

POPPIES

In 1915, Moina Michael, a teacher from Georgia, read "In Flanders Fields." A Canadian military doctor named John McCrae wrote the poem. The poem is about the rows of poppies growing between the graves on a battlefield in Flanders, Belgium. Mrs. Michael wrote her own poem titled "We Shall Keep the Faith." She wrote about wearing poppies to remember fallen soldiers. Today, the poppy is worn as a symbol of remembrance.

MEMORIALS

Memorials honoring fallen soldiers are found across the United States. Many have been built in Washington, D.C. One example is the African American Civil War Memorial. A sculpture named "The Spirit of Freedom" is on display at this memorial. One side of the sculpture is carved with the image of a family as the son leaves to join the war. The other side of the sculpture is carved with the images of three soldiers and a sailor.

A Song to Remember

The United States National Anthem, *The Star-Spangled Banner*, is sung at Memorial Day celebrations across the country.

Oh, say, can you see, by the dawn's early light,

What so proudly we hailed at the twilight's last gleaming?

Whose broad stripes and bright stars, thru the perilous fight,

O'er the ramparts we watched, were so gallantly streaming!

And the rockets' red glare, the bombs bursting in air,

Gave proof through the night that our flag was still there.

O say, does that star-spangled banner yet wave

O'er the land of the free and the home of the brave?

Francis Scott Key

Write Your Own Song

Songwriting is a fun way to express thoughts and ideas.
Get creative, and write your own song.

Listen to a song that you like and pay attention to the lyrics. Which words rhyme? How many verses are there? How many lines are in each verse? How many times is the chorus sung?

Start brainstorming ideas. What do you want your song to be about? Choose an event, idea, person, or feeling you would like to write about.

Write the verses. Songs usually have three or four verses. Each one will be different but should relate to the chorus.

Come up with music for your song. Some songwriters like to write the music before the words. Others will write them at the same time.

Many songwriters work with other people to create songs. Try working with a classmate or friend to think of a tune or words for your song.

Write the chorus to your song. The chorus is the main idea of the song. It connects the verses together.

Fingerpaint Flag

There are many fun crafts you can create for Memorial Day, such as a fingerpaint flag.

Red Paint

White Paint

Blue Paint

Mural Paper

4 Easy Steps to Complete Your Flag

1 Take a large piece of mural paper, and paint a blue square in the upper left corner.

2 Paint white stars on the blue square.

3 Use your hands to paint red stripes across the rest of the flag.

4 When the mural paper is dry, hang up your flag.

Memorial Day Salad

Ingredients

1/2 cup soft cream cheese
1/2 cup mayonnaise
1/2 pound miniature
   marshmallows, diced
1 cup chopped pecans

1/2 cup chopped fruit, such
   as pineapple, oranges, cherries,
   or grapes, well drained
1 dash salt
1 cup whipping cream, whipped stiff
sprinkle of coconut

Equipment

medium-sized bowl
wooden spoon
knife

spatula
large pan

Directions

1. Blend the cream cheese and mayonnaise in a medium-sized bowl.
2. Add the marshmallows, fruit, pecans, and salt.
3. Lightly fold in the cream.
4. Pour into the large pan.
5. Chill overnight.
6. Sprinkle coconut on top, and serve.

Test Your Knowledge!

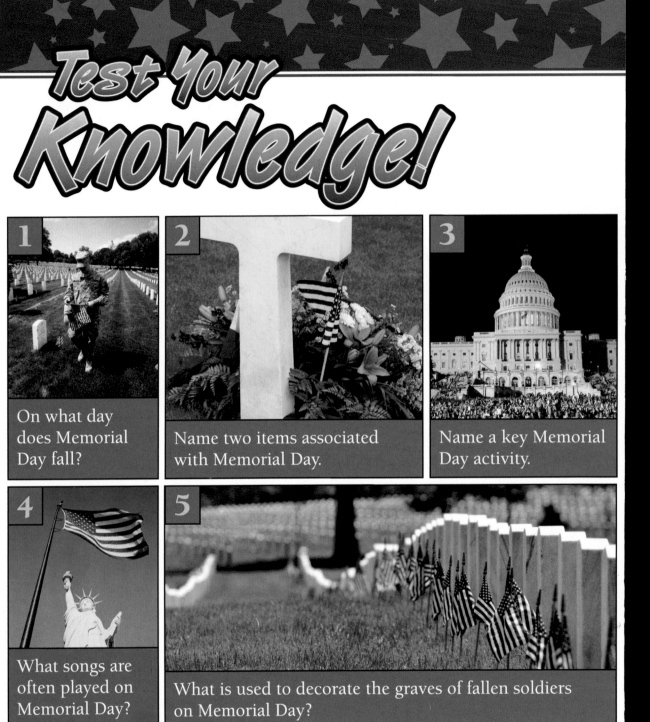

1

On what day does Memorial Day fall?

2

Name two items associated with Memorial Day.

3

Name a key Memorial Day activity.

4

What songs are often played on Memorial Day?

5

What is used to decorate the graves of fallen soldiers on Memorial Day?

Quiz Answers:
1. Memorial Day falls on the last Monday in May.
2. Flowers and flags are two items associated with Memorial Day.
3. Most people bring flowers to the cemetery on Memorial Day.
4. "Taps" and "The Star-Spangled Banner" are often played at Memorial Day ceremonies.
5. The graves of fallen soldiers are decorated with flowers and small American flags.

Glossary

Arlington National Cemetery: one of the largest cemeteries in the United States; located in Virginia, most of the people who died during the Civil War are buried here

comrades: soldiers and other military members who served in times of war

Confederate: the southern states of the Civil War

half-staff: a flag lowered about halfway down the flagpole to show respect for the dead

leis: flower necklaces

monuments: objects built in remembrance of a person, place, or event

patriotic: showing love for one's country

"Taps": a military song that is usually played on a trumpet or bugle

Union: the northern states of the Civil War

veterans: people who have served in the armed forces

vow: a promise or pledge

Index

Log on to www.av2books.com

AV² by Weigl brings you media enhanced books that support active learning. Go to **www.av2books.com**, and enter the special code inside the front cover of this book. You will gain access to enriched and enhanced content that supplements and complements this book. Content includes video, audio, web links, quizzes, a slide show, and activities.

Audio
Listen to sections of
the book read aloud.

Video
Watch informative video clips.

Web Link
Find research sites and
play interactive games.

Try This!
Complete activities and
hands-on experiments.

WHAT'S ONLINE?

Try This! Complete activities and hands-on experiments.	**Web Link** Find research sites and play interactive games.	**Video** Watch informative video clips.	**EXTRA FEATURES**
Pages 8-9 Write a biography about an important person	Pages 6-7 Find out more about the history of Memorial Day	Pages 4-5 Watch a video about Memorial Day	**Audio** Hear introductory au at the top of every p
Pages 10-11 Describe the features and special events of a similar celebration around the world	Pages 10-11 Learn more about similar celebrations around the world	Pages 12-13 Check out a video about how people celebrate Memorial Day	**Key Words** Study vocabulary, and play a matching word game.
Pages 14-15 Complete a mapping activity about Memorial Day celebrations	Pages 16-17 Find information about important holiday symbols		**Slide Show** View images and captions, and try a writing activity.
Pages 16-17 Try this activity about important holiday symbols	Pages 18-19 Link to more information about Memorial Day		**AV² Quiz** Take this quiz to test your knowledge
Pages 20-21 Play an interactive activity	Pages 20-21 Check out more holiday craft ideas		